Tell Me WHY

EARTH
Questions and Answers

by
Rebecca Phillips-Bartlett

BEARPORT
PUBLISHING

Minneapolis, Minnesota

Credits
All images are courtesy of Shutterstock.com, unless otherwise specified. With thanks to Getty Images, Thinkstock Photo, iStockphoto, and Adobe Stock.

Cover – Orgus88, BNP Design Studio, Aliva, Perfectorius, Gaidamashchuk, hancreative_id, ilnazgilov, ivector, Marko Petrushevski, mentalmind, Pretty woman, Tartila, Zozo Kharitonova. Throughout BNP Design Studio, Orgus88, Perfectorius, Aliva. 4–5 – kotomiti, igoriss, nemchinowa. 6–7 – Talented Bee, wannawit_vck, kostab. 8–9 – Arif_Vector, kuroksta, onyx124. 10–11 – Runrun2, Iconic Bestiary, victoriap_107, Coldimages. 12–13 – Colorfuel Studio, Godline, LAUDiseno, Hayri Er, Mulad Images. 14–15 – alexandrabadashovaa, YummyBuum, hapabapa. 16–17 – Leene, robuart, Colorfuel Studio, Kavic.C, Natalia Sheinkin, Marc Guyt. 18–19 – Daria Pozhilova, Inkoly, janrysavy. 20–21 – Amanita Silvicora, GinaVector, Rumka vodki, Neliakott, WilleeCole. 22–23 – Jacob Wackerhausen, TPopova.

Bearport Publishing Company Product Development Team
Publisher: Jen Jenson; Director of Product Development: Spencer Brinker; Managing Editor: Allison Juda; Editor: Cole Nelson; Associate Editor: Naomi Reich; Associate Editor: Tiana Tran; Art Director: Colin O'Dea; Designer: Kim Jones; Designer: Kayla Eggert; Product Development Specialist: Owen Hamlin

Library of Congress Cataloging-in-Publication Data is available at www.loc.gov or upon request from the publisher.

ISBN: 979-8-89232-758-9 (hardcover)
ISBN: 979-8-89232-954-5 (paperback)
ISBN: 979-8-89232-845-6 (ebook)

© 2025 BookLife Publishing
This edition is published by arrangement with BookLife Publishing.

North American adaptations © 2025 Bearport Publishing Company. All rights reserved. No part of this publication may be reproduced in whole or in part, stored in any retrieval system, or transmitted in any form or by any means, electronic, mechanical, photocopying, recording, or otherwise, without written permission from the publisher.

For more information, write to Bearport Publishing, 5357 Penn Avenue South, Minneapolis, MN 55419.

Contents

Tell Me Why 4
Why Are Deserts So Dry? 6
Why Is Antarctica So Cold? 7
Why Is the Sky Blue? 8
Why Do Rainbows Appear? 10
Why Do the Leaves Drop Off Some Trees? 11
Why Does It Rain? 12
Why Does It Snow? 13
Why Do Earthquakes Happen? 14
Why Do Some Rocks Have Layers? 16
Why Is the Sea Salty? 17
Why Do Oceans Have Tides? 18
Why Is Mud Different Colors? 20
Why Do Volcanoes Erupt? 21
Asking Questions 22
Glossary 24
Index 24

TELL ME WHY

Earth is a wonderful planet with many interesting features. From wild weather to colorful stones, every part of Earth has a story to tell.

Earth is always changing. Sometimes, the things that happen seem strange. There are so many things about Earth that leave us wondering **WHY?**

QUESTION
What questions do you have about Earth?

WHY ARE DESERTS SO DRY?

The **equator** around the center of Earth gets the most sunlight of any area on the planet. As the sun shines down, hot and wet air rises up into the sky. This causes a lot of rain to fall. The air dries out as it moves away from the equator. So, the areas just north and south of the equator get less rain. They become dry deserts.

FUN FACT
Some deserts are hot and sandy, while others are cold and icy.

WHY IS ANTARCTICA SO COLD?

Antarctica is at the bottom of the planet. Because of this, it doesn't get direct sunlight. This light hits the area at an angle, which means it must travel farther through the air. By the time it reaches Antarctica, the light is too weak to warm the area much.

FUN FACT
Antarctica doesn't get any sunlight for about six months of the year.

Another reason for the cold is ice! Antarctica is covered by the largest ice sheet on Earth. This helps keep the air very cold.

WHY IS THE SKY BLUE?

The sky looks blue because of how sunlight moves through Earth's **atmosphere**. Sunlight is made up of all the colors of the rainbow. As the light passes through the atmosphere, it gets scattered. The blue light is scattered more than other colors, making the sky appear blue.

FUN FACT
Red, orange, and yellow light take longer to scatter through the atmosphere.

At sunrise and sunset, the sky sometimes looks red and orange. This is because the sun is lower in the sky, so the light has to travel through more of Earth's atmosphere. During this longer journey, most of the blue light is scattered out of the way. The result is that we see more orange and red.

WHY DO RAINBOWS APPEAR?

Rainbows happen when sunlight passes through raindrops at just the right angle. The light bends and is split apart inside the water. When light exits the raindrops, it has been separated into all its different colors. This creates a rainbow.

QUESTION
Have you ever seen a rainbow?

WHY DO THE LEAVES DROP OFF SOME TREES?

A leaf's job is to turn water and sunlight into food for the tree. However, this is difficult to do during colder months because there isn't as much sunlight or liquid water. The trees drop their leaves since they can no longer make food.

FUN FACT
Trees that lose their leaves for winter are called **deciduous** (dih-SID-yoo-uhs) trees.

WHY DOES IT RAIN?

Clouds are made of tiny water droplets. Inside the clouds, the water droplets join together and get bigger. When they become too heavy to stay up inside the clouds, they fall to the ground as rain.

WHY DOES IT SNOW?

When water gets very cold, it freezes. If the **temperature** inside a cloud is cold enough, tiny water droplets freeze and turn into ice. More water freezes onto the ice and it becomes a snowflake. Once the flake is too heavy to stay in the cloud, it falls to the ground as snow.

FUN FACT
Every snowflake is different!

WHY DO EARTHQUAKES HAPPEN?

An earthquake is when underground movements make the ground shake.

Earth has many layers. The outer layer is made up of large slabs of rock called **tectonic plates**. These plates are always moving very slowly.

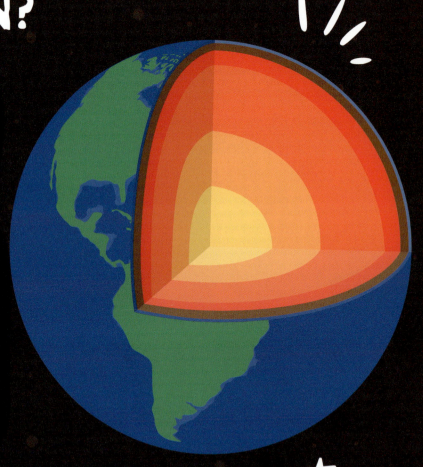

Sometimes, tectonic plates get stuck against one another. The rocks, however, continue to push. When they finally slip free, the sudden movement makes the shaking we call an earthquake.

FUN FACT
Earthquakes can be powerful enough to make the ground crack.

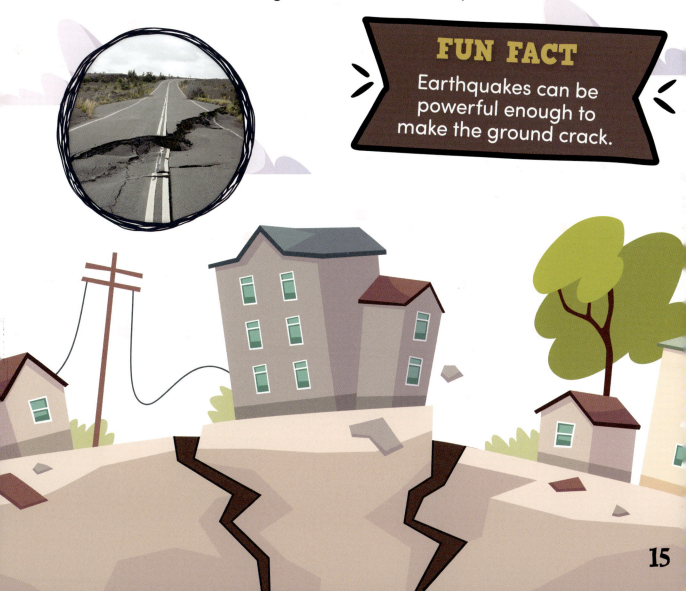

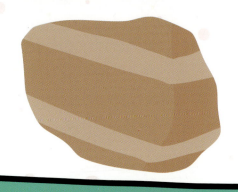

FUN FACT
There are three main types of rocks on Earth.

WHY DO SOME ROCKS HAVE LAYERS?

There are a couple reasons rocks may have layers. Some layers are formed when sand and mud pile up over thousands of years. The layers are squashed down under more layers and eventually turn into rock. Other rocks form layers under extreme heat. The heat causes the different **minerals** in the rocks to separate into different layers.

WHY IS THE SEA SALTY?

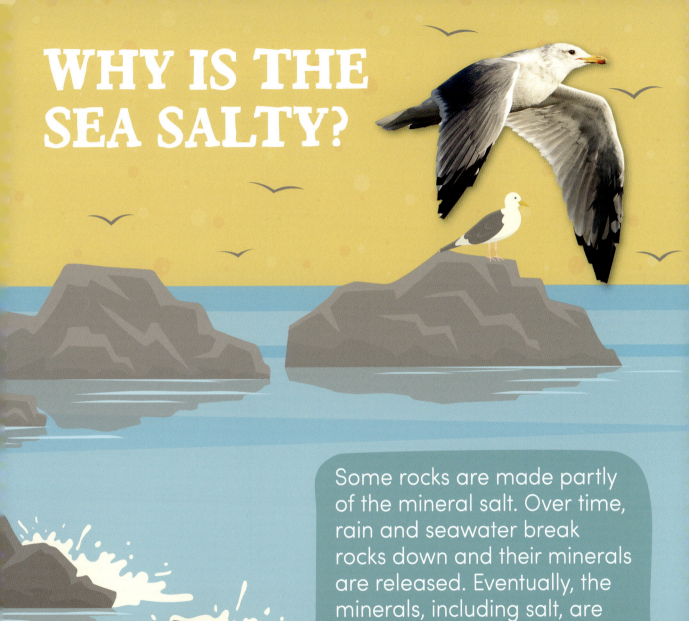

Some rocks are made partly of the mineral salt. Over time, rain and seawater break rocks down and their minerals are released. Eventually, the minerals, including salt, are carried into the ocean. This makes the sea salty.

WHY DO OCEANS HAVE TIDES?

The oceans have tides because of the moon's **gravity**. Gravity is the force that pulls objects toward one another. The bigger the object, the more pull it has. As the moon travels around Earth, its gravity pulls on the planet, including the water.

FUN FACT
Tides are easiest to see on beaches. However, they happen in the open ocean, too.

The moon's gravity pulls strongest on the water on the side of Earth that is facing the moon. Water rises on the opposite side of Earth, too. These rises are called high tides. On other parts of the planet, the water levels are lower. They are at low tide. As Earth spins and the moon moves around the planet, the tides change.

19

WHY IS MUD DIFFERENT COLORS?

Mud is a mix of water and soil. It gets its color from the different **materials** in the soil, such as rocks, minerals, and plants. The different types and amounts of these materials in mud change the color. Mud can be brown, red, green, black, and more.

WHY DO VOLCANOES ERUPT?

Volcanoes are openings in Earth's crust where superhot melted rock escapes. This liquid rock, called **magma**, forms deep underground. As it rises to the surface, gas bubbles form, and they create lots of **pressure**. Eventually, this pressure pushes the hot rock through volcanoes, causing them to erupt.

FUN FACT
Once magma is above ground, it is called lava.

Asking Questions

This book is full of questions you might have had about Earth. How do we know the answers? Because many people before you have asked the same things.

Asking questions is a great way to learn about the world around you. There are still so many interesting things to discover about Earth. So, stay curious, and keep asking questions!

QUESTION
What other questions do you have about Earth?

23

Glossary

atmosphere the layers of gases that make up the air surrounding Earth

deciduous having leaves that fall off every year

equator the imaginary line around Earth that is halfway between the North and the South Poles

gravity a powerful force that pulls objects toward one another

magma hot, liquid rock beneath Earth's surface

materials substances that things are made of

minerals solid substances not from living things that can be found in nature

pressure a force made by pushing on something

tectonic plates huge pieces of rock that make up Earth's outer crust

temperature how hot or cold something is

volcanoes openings in Earth's crust that can erupt to let out lava and gases

Index

colors 4, 8, 10, 20
equator 6
gravity 18–19
leaves 11
magma 21
minerals 16–17, 20
moon 18–19
rock 14–17, 20–21
sunlight 6–8, 10–11
tectonic plates 14–15
tides 18–19
water 10–13, 17–20